PUSH · PULL EMPTY · FULL

A BOOK OF OPPOSITES BY TANA HOBAN

MACMILLAN PUBLISHING CO., INC.

NEW YORK

Macmillan Publishing Co., Inc.
866 Third Avenue, New York, N.Y. 10022
Collier Macmillan Canada Ltd.

Library of Congress catalog card number: 72-90410

Printed in the United States of America

10   9   8   7   6   5

The photographs in this book were taken with
two cameras: the Beseler Topcon RE Super D
(35mm) with 58mm and 135mm lenses, and the
Hasselblad 500C (2¼″ x 2¼″) with Planar 80mm
f2.8 lens. The films used were Plus-X and Tri-X,
developed in Ethol UFG and printed on Varigam
paper in Dektol developer.

This one is for Susan

push

pull

empty

full

dry

in

out

up

down

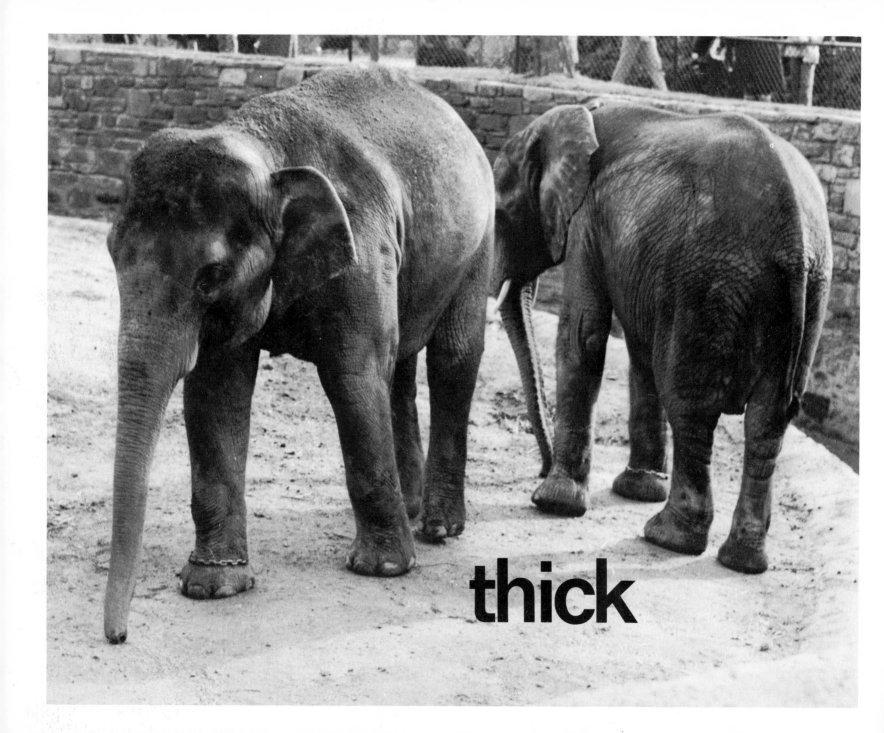

thick

thin

whole

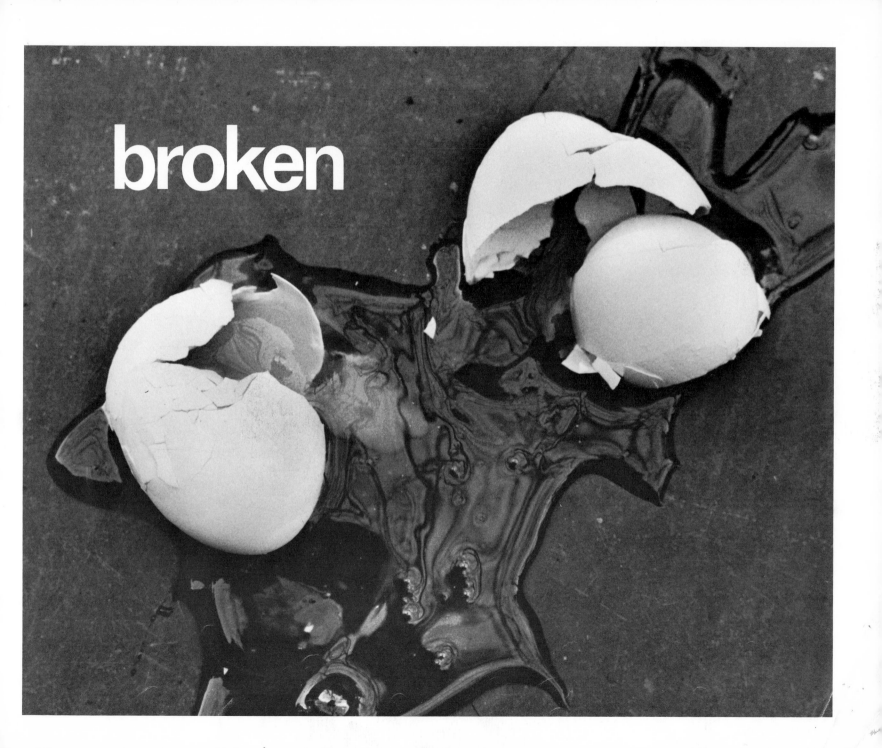

back

big

little

last

many

few

heavy

light

together

apart

left

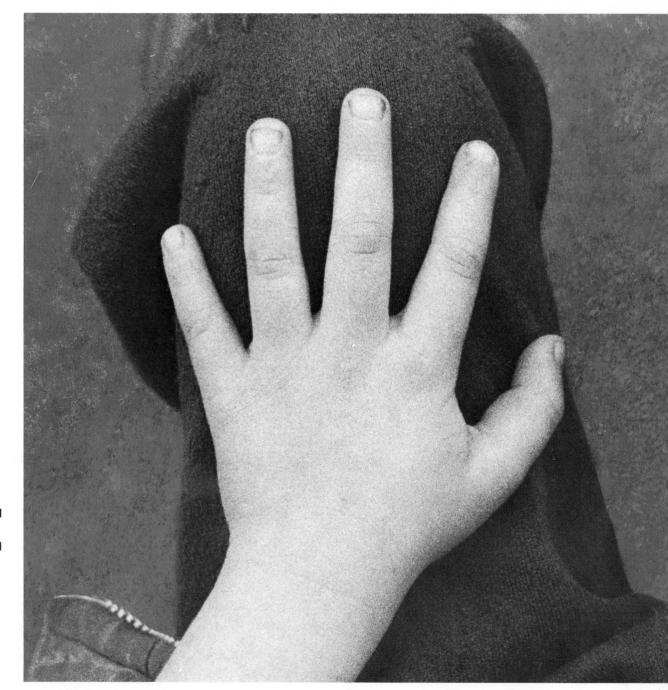

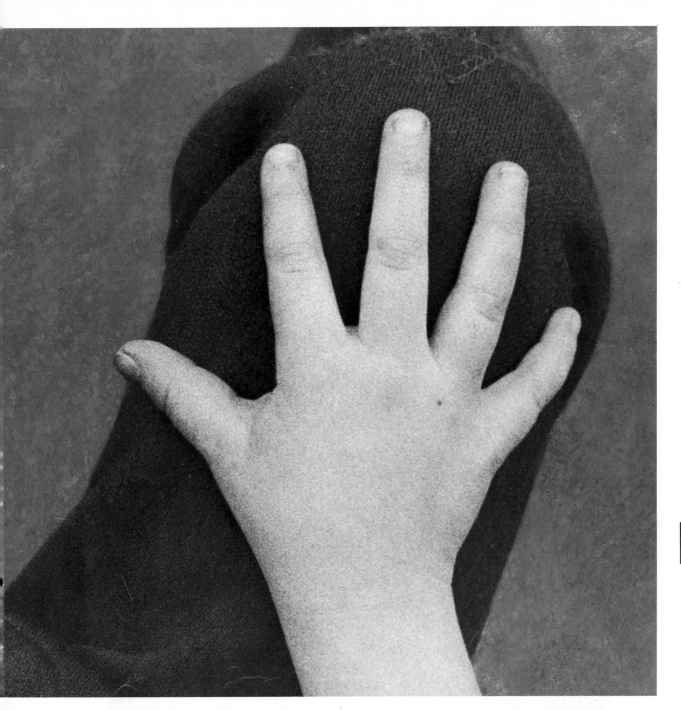

right

day